Word Hot

Word Hot

Mary Meriam

HEADMISTRESS PRESS

Cover art by Mary Delany. Amaryllis Belladonna (Hexandria
Monogynia), from an album (Vol.I, 30); Lily Daffodil.
1775 Collage of coloured papers, with bodycolour and
watercolour, on black ink background © Trustees of the
British Museum

Cover & book design by Mary Meriam

PUBLISHER
Headmistress Press
60 Shipview Lane
Sequim, WA 98382
Telephone: 917-428-8312
Email: headmistresspress@gmail.com
Website: headmistresspress.blogspot.com

With deepest gratitude,
this book is dedicated to
Lillian Faderman

Contents

Who leaves me rootless

You! all rich now? man at your cozy table,
tête-à-tête, now gets every murmur, whisper,
laugh and sigh that dreamily leaves your lips? How
sweetly your echo

slays my heart, my hard-ridden heart, that beating
harder, horse-whipped, stifles my voice. Now wordless,
bee-stung, broke, deserted, I look at you and
totally lose it.

Fire snakes and slithers, now blisters blazing
skin, now eyes lose eyesight, now eardrums beat drums,
sweating rain, now race in a thunder tremble
whirlwind tornado

green as grass I'm taken, a prisoner chained in
ravaged daisies. Where is my mind, my flower—
petal-plucked and rootless. Be brave now Mary,
dirt poor but healthy.

Lesbian Studies

O my muse, promiscuous muse, my bunny,
hop off paper, hop in my arms, my darling
muse not mine, my everyone muse, please let me
touch and amuse you.

Now the past is sliding away, past harm's way,
past the nightmare hidden in sex's dream, when
you, in need, decided to strip and show your
body to die for.

Naked, word hot, here are your breasts, *I'm breathless
writing this, yes throbbing and flushed,* your memoir's
pictures move me far from a text perusal,
write me, I'm lovesick.

Mountain Town

Dear morning moon above

                    the crumbling stairs

a precious book

            a landing where I raise

my eyes to see you,

              make me understand

the steps to take to you

                here in the trees

the tiny castle built

                of old gray stone

the stairs so steep and cracked

                  the day so young

the doors still locked   I wait

                I breathe

                        I find

the shadow of the biggest tree

                for shade.

Another trip,

              across the morning sky

a jet drags two thin streams

                of ghostly cloud

a path I think you take

              so far above me.

Inevitable flower blooms

                alone

naked, pink, and tall:

            one Naked Lady.

I read and borrow

              borrow, read

                    return.

To Lillian

Some summer nights, it seems like you are mine,
a lilly dream grown out of loneliness,
when all my sepals, stems, and petals pine,
and I can almost hear you saying yes.
But no, your flower bed is closely tended.
There's nothing you can do with my bouquet.
The past and all its sorrows have been mended;
likewise, my lilly dream should fade away.
Should fade away as summer flowers fade,
petal by petal falling to the ground,
singing a sad and lonely serenade,
wilted and dizzy, lost and strewn around.
It seems the lilly dream is mine to keep,
pressed tight inside these pages, fast asleep.

Portrait of a Woman Revealing Her Breasts

Sensing Tintoretto's brushes
on her breasts, tender, luscious,
she looks away and faintly blushes.

Can we understand the deal
she made to model and reveal?
Was it for love? Oh, let me feel

this love, then let my fingers slide
along each folded, flowing side
of parted dress and salty tide,

until I touch her strands of pearls.
Now tickled by her auburn curls
and wavy locks, her image twirls

an ocean where I cannot swim
and flailing, drown. Here on the slim
shore of sound, I sigh and limn.

Avifauna

Somewhere in the world tonight,
    someone waits for me;
her red silk slippers of delight,
    her blue room by the sea,

her tangerines, her house of words,
    her tragedy and play,
seem close as all these singing birds,
    and likewise, far away.

Personal Ad

Lap me
        languish me
                lake my longing
Here on earth
        no gunshots, no hunger.

Dreamworld of eyelids relaxing
Earlobes receptive to sound

You across the table, looking at me
You in the hammock, the bath, the bed

Walking the fields on the swallowtail path,
Wounded but alive, pulsing with courage.

Let me touch her. Let her be you.

Wedding Song for Two Women

Didn't I always know this leaf
in some cathedral in my mind
impossibly high with green relief
was with me intertwined?

Wasn't it her inside my book,
the queen of chance and understanding,
and wasn't she why I undertook
my painted look at landing?

Oh, falling this way, the light, the air,
this feeling through the atmosphere,
this holding her hand and kissing her there,
without her being near

the saddest edge of the spinning world,
this knowing and never knowing before
the stems and vines of longing curled
around her open door.

Eau Sauvage

Two windows weeping lilac curtains, sheer
and long, and lilac bushes perfume air
from snowy peaks. A quiet room, austere.
A mattress on the floor, a desk and chair.

The disco dancers throbbing in the dark,
drinking and drunk. Speed shots of burning light.
I go there. Why then does this woman park
herself in front of me and break the night?

Her eau sauvage for men. Her downcast eyes.
Her short black hair. *Intoxicate my mind,*
Professor. Say your body tells no lies.
Loosen your full white bosom from its bind.

At last seduced, I kiss her on the lips.
Again, again, the driving downbeat whips.

Cave In

The forest sighs for succulent romance.
The moonlight jiggles in a modern dance.
The waiting window holds the weary tree.
The midnight branches tap. Come back to me.
My bed of fallen needles scares the crow.
My frost left all the crickets in distress.
My earth is certain nothing green can grow.
The threads get weaker in my careless dress,
and I have lost the will and way to sew.

The Woman of My Dreams

At last, the hour strikes to go to sleep.
She waits for me—there's no one else. Her face,
at first, reflects the moon, then her embrace
embroiders cloaks to hide the very deep.

As I begin to fall to sleep, I reap
the whole day's dreams. My sleep is wearing lace.
She lullabies me to a calmer place,
then fastens me with pearls and lets me weep.

Night

Darling night, again I address your distance,
cricket racket, owl on the prowl, the letter
Z in bubbles, blankets and sheets, your pillow
          making me heavy,

oh, the wait for you to undo your buttons,
let your swiftness go through the open window,
moonward while the weight of you stays, unfolds, and
          blooms with an orchid's

sweet-sick scent; but when you descend on me, good-
night, the distant fire arrives and takes me
down with you, much deeper than sense, to private
          radiant oceans.

An Entering

I am asleep on my city's dead street,
when you take my hand, and then we are walking;
there is silence, but I can feel your hand talking,
pulling me deeper into your warm, sweet
language, speaking to me, with a teacher's eloquence,
of your need, which is beginning to dawn on me
in the dark theater, where no one can see
the tutorial of your kisses, which are kindling the sense
of warmer and closer things yet to be known—
how could I then awaken, hideous, alone?

Melon Balls

What do I know of sex in my seclusion,
the big black bull outside the hot barbed wire,
the female rancher's sweat in the confusion,
for all I know, the bad bull's balls on fire?
I'm most familiar with my quiet table,
with casseroles, with roasted nuts and seeds,
with stewing beans, with salads cool and stable,
with satisfying simple daily needs.
A smooth-skinned melon? Yes, it fits my hands.
I feel the melon's soft warm weight and think
of her. A lizard nods. He understands?
I rinse the melon in the kitchen sink
and try to let my thoughts run down the drain.
The absence of her pleasure is my pain.

Country Music

It was because I dreamed of you again,
and soggy leaves were sticking to my shoes,
and I was tired of listening to men,
that you again seemed closer than a muse.
I went outside to catch a breath of air,
the wind blew in my face like a surprise,
warmer for fall, it seemed, than it was fair,
but colder air was lurking in disguise.
And all around my mind, the monstrous dome
of heaven clings to hell beneath my feet,
choosing which way I walk away from home,
kicking the leaves, as if my incomplete
existence could be saved without you near,
as if a wish could make a muse appear.

Port of Call

Nothing but touch will ever satisfy
my storming surge of lust for you.

Appear

dikes moan.

Come near

waves lash.

Come close

gulls cry.

My burning vessel flaunts the flag sincere.

Way to the west, my rusty bark is sighted,
though lately stuck in piddling inland lakes.
Her signal flares

Condition Unrequited

yet see the spray her bonny bow shape makes.

My wish runs whistling through the dusky air,
laden with galley-cook and sailor cries,
to gaze at the blue, blue sky of your sultry eyes,
and sniff your wavy, salty spring of hair,
to find the smooth pink shell of your perfect ear
and breathe
            it's you
                    it's you I want
come here.

Thought in a Heat Wave

The words, the books, the strain,
the loneliness, the pain,
the beast of woe, the lion roar,
it doesn't matter anymore

because I have a thought,
tamed, soothed, caught:
the poetry I said to you,
the lines that led to you,

the arteries around my heart,
the words I read to you,
the breath and rhymes, the breathing in,
the us not dead to you,

the dancing of you in my dreams;
I could be wed to you;
my loveline veering off my palm
could go, instead, to you;

your jewel burning in my mind,
your brilliant cry, so kind,
your evening sky of cobalt blue,
yes, I think of you

and I together in one place,
with time and room to sigh,
and moved by magic to embrace
the body, you and I.

Thoughts

Some thoughts are too unbearable to think,
but still they rock me nightly, tidal waves
of worry, thoughts that knock me off the brink,
drown me, and bury me in shapeless caves.
Some thoughts are faces I once knew, and some
remember voices, visions, trouble, thunder,
and some thoughts dwell on what I have become,
and others flutter from the world with wonder.

I keep one thought apart from all the rest,
safe in a locket on a silver chain
around my neck, close to my pulsing breast,
my one thought safe from salty spray and rain
that soak my aspirations through and through.
Drown me again. My thought holds on to you.

So Close

O did I not? Yes soe did I
Mary Sidney

The owl so close, I see her fine
feathers of gold. She doesn't seem
to mind the snow. I see snow shine
like glitter on her coat, and dream
of you at my front door tonight,
like magic through the foot of snow,
or did you glide here and alight?
You step inside, we say hello,
then kissing you, I slide to the floor,
and every inch of you, adore.

But thou wilt not, nor he will not
Shakespeare

But now you have no time for me?
But who was I for all this time?
But is there someone I could be
so you would stay by me? Or I'm
not good enough, nor quick to change?
Tighter and tighter gets the knot
that binds you to this interchange?
You feel you've given all you've got?
But I grow roses in the snow
for you, so please, oh please don't go.

iMuse iMoan

please take me with you when you go
there's no one else i've asked this of
my darling muse i miss you so
please take me with you when you go
as light as air as still as love
a tiny pocket message glow

Anticipation's sweet

Anticipation's sweet, so shall we go there?
Here is my proposition apropos there.

You witness this, the book of my seclusion,
rollicking from my tongue, the words aglow there.

I watch your contrails through my windowpane,
the curtain parted for the distant show there.

And in this deep disturbance of my sleep,
a figure much like yours is dancing slow there.

Thicker and thicker honeysuckle vines,
sweeter and sweeter blossoms seem to grow there.

I make my little plans for future kisses—
there I begin, and there, until I know there.

The roundness of your chin, quite merciless.
Faint humming of a bee beneath the snow there.

Muse of To

To go somewhere, to drive a car, to fly,
to take a train or bus, go north or south,
or east or west, to hear your sounds, to cry
at words like music spilling from your mouth,
this fantasy, so simple, I could dream
through Russian tundra, down the city street,
through farmers' fields, across the frozen stream,
past fallen trees, away from my retreat.
To climb, to slip, to fall, to walk, to run,
to use my legs and feet to leap divides,
to ride the freeways, cloverleafs, the one
deserted road, until the daylight slides
to night, and like the pillow for your head,
to bring you all the words that should be said.

Acknowledgments

My thanks to the editors of the following publications, in which these poems appeared, sometimes in earlier versions:

Amsterdam Quarterly: "Mountain Town"
Autumn Sky Poetry: "Portrait of a Woman Revealing Her Breasts"
Horizon Review: "An Entering"
Kin Poetry Journal: "Thought in a Heat Wave"
Light Quarterly: "iMuse iMoan," "Avifauna"
Literary Imagination: "Who leaves me rootless"
Mezzo Cammin: "To Lillian"
Phati'tude Literary Magazine: "Portrait of a Woman Revealing Her Breasts"
Rhythm Poetry Magazine: "Eau Sauvage," "Anticipation's sweet"
Sixty-Six: The Journal of Sonnet Studies: "Melon Balls"
The Brooklyner: "Night"
The Evansville Review: "Country Music"
The Gay & Lesbian Review: "Personal Ad," "The Woman of My Dreams"
Windy City Times: "Lesbian Studies"

Anthologies
Here Come the Brides! Love and Marriage Lesbian-Style (Seal Press, 2012): "Wedding Song for Two Women"
Hot Sonnets (Entasis Press, 2011): "Melon Balls"
Lady Business (Sibling Rivalry Press, 2012): "Melon Balls," "An Entering," "Portrait of a Woman Revealing Her Breasts," "Eau Sauvage"

www.ingramcontent.com/pod-product-compliance
Lightning Source LLC
Chambersburg PA
CBHW070048070426
42449CB00012BA/3187